The Gap

Written by Caroline Green

Collins

a map

. . . .

kit in a sack

a map

kit in a sack

a dog

a gap

a dog

a gap

man

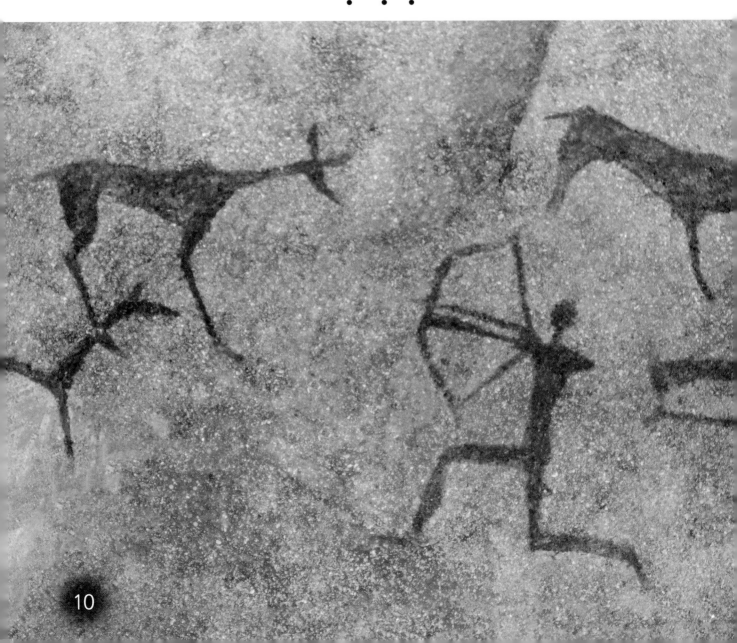

dots
· · · ·

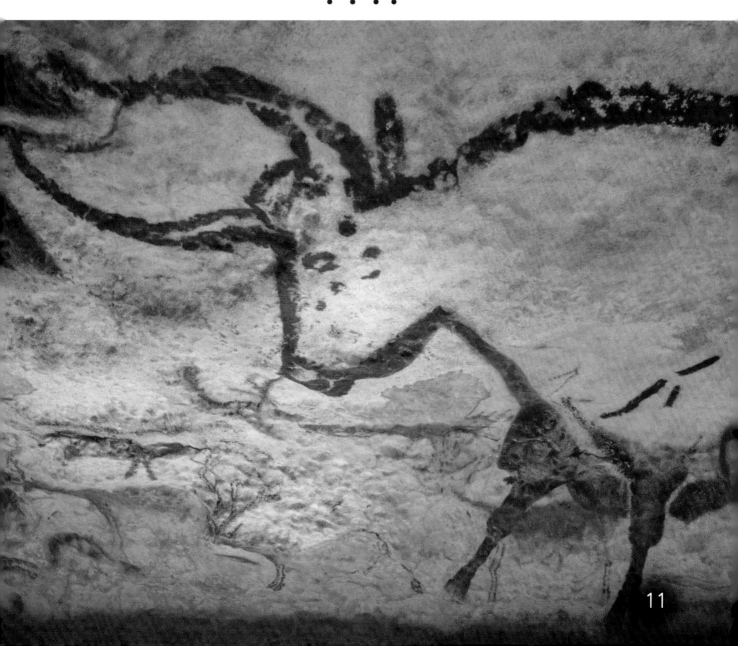

man

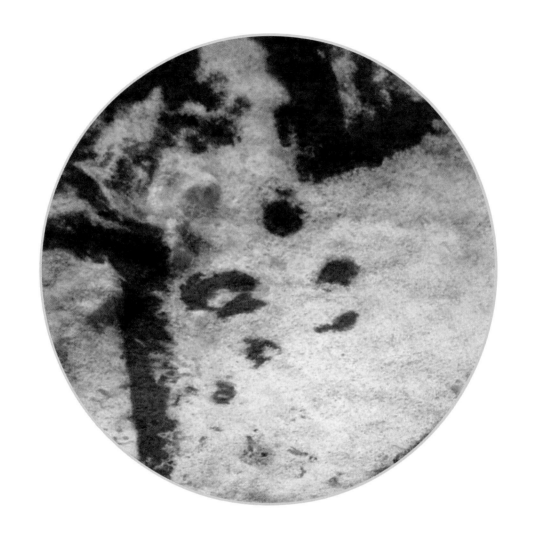

dots

/o/

14

15

Review: After reading

Use your assessment from hearing the children read to choose any GPCs, words or tricky words that need additional practice.

Read 1: Decoding

- Use grapheme cards to make any words you need to practise. Model reading those words, using teacher-led blending.
- Look at the "I spy sounds" pages (14–15) together. Ask the children to point out as many things as they can in the picture that begin with the /o/ sound. (*otter, octopus, orange, olives*) Repeat for the /d/ sound. (*deer, ducks, dragonflies, dog, daisies, dish, drink*)
- Ask the children to follow as you read the whole book, demonstrating fluency and prosody.

Read 2: Vocabulary

- Look back through the book and discuss the pictures. Encourage the children to talk about details that stand out for them. Use a dialogic talk model to expand on their ideas and recast them in full sentences as naturally as possible.
- Work together to expand vocabulary by naming objects in the pictures that children do not know.
- On page 5, which word tells us what is inside the sack? (*kit*) What things might the kit include? (e.g. *water, phone, raincoat, torch*)

Read 3: Comprehension

- Reread pages 4 to 7. Ask: Where did the dog and person go? (e.g. *through the gap, into the cave*) Do you think they planned the trip? Why? (e.g. *yes, because they took a map and their kit*)
- Turn to pages 10 and 11. Ask questions about the pictures. For example: Where are these pictures? (e.g. *inside the gap, in the cave*) What animals can you see? (e.g. *deer, bison*)